THE NEW WAY FOR AFRICAN RELATIONSHIPS

HOW THE AFRICAN COMMUNITY CAN EMBRACE ITS PAST AND ITS FUTURE

By Valerie Muzelenga

To my father, mother and my Siblings and extended family. To my husband, our child, and grandchildren, with all my Love. Thank you for urging me on to carry on writing and realise my dream.

INTRODUCTION

———————

"I wrote this book to draw the best from both Africa and the west to educate those who have lost their way in the merging of cultures and to give them hope for themselves, their families, their children, and their community."

In many ways we facing a crisis in our African communities: our immersion in western traditions has resulted in skyrocketing divorce, struggling and disrespectful children, the loss of culture and identity and men and women battling to love and be loved.

Our great African heritage of teachings and traditions holds answers to many of these problems and can help to heal broken relationships.

Accordingly, some traditions and perspectives of the west also have value for healthy relationships.

Valerie Muzelenga is a respected African counsellor and elder and has drawn from years of experience in both western and African cultures to write this valuable guidebook for people wanting happier families, communities, and relationships. It not only details the positive traditions of our past but also demonstrates how these can be applied to our future.

The *New Way for African Relationships* is a must read book for people looking for answers to their relationship problems and for those who want to make their relationships even better.

FOREWORD

———

*"'Cultural integration' is key to our peaceful and progressive
co-habitation of our world"*

When a mutual friend of the author and mine recommended
me to write the forward for this book, she sure knew what she
was doing. It was not because she knew I had done forwards and
edited other books excellently in the past, it was more because
she sensed the fact that I would have a great connection with
this particular piece of work and hence be able to write it off or
recommend it in my usual frank manner.

Dr. Ava Eagle Brown, must have figured that my combined
experiences being an Obstetrician and Gynaecologist, a passionate
Motivational Speaker, Women and Youth Reproductive Health

Advocate as well as a Social Entrepreneur and Blogger must count for something. However, most importantly, also being a Nigerian raised on the African continent who has spent the last 10 years in the United Kingdom, must have struck her as a good exposure that gives me a holistic background to vet this book for an authenticity signature or not that will direct any reader.

I recommend this book to every one irrespective of age, gender or race, who wishes to connect with the difficult subject of identity, relationships and a merging of cultures in today's global village – our world.

As we each crisscross continents and settle in new communities, challenges arise in associations, life and love. "Cultural shocks" like the one I endured when I first arrived in the United Kingdom many years ago can be confidence sapping, identity distorting and relationships non- facilitating. One therefore needs a good dose of resilience and inspiration to keep things together especially as an African female irrespective of which role we find our selves.

This book by Valerie Muzelenga is one very valuable resource we all need in our arsenal to enable us acquire the nuggets of wisdom required to navigate this difficult terrain. Her years of experience, evolving over from being a Registered Nurse and Midwife to an excellent Marriage and Relationship Counsellor, Mentor, Inspirational Speaker, Author as well as women empowerment champion who grew up in Zambia and has lived a substantial number of years in the United Kingdom, all rolled into one is all packed into this book.

In this book Valerie outlines the strength and beauty of the Zambian culture and life style while she has the honesty to acknowledge the perceived defects and imperfection therein and how westernisation, immigration and migration is affecting our core values of identity, relationship, marriage and living in general. She goes on to proffer solutions to these challenges.

Within the pages of this volume, which I could not put down from when I started it till I got to the end, she questions how women can ensure that they are not in a place of submission. In her words, the solution is that "it is essential women communicate their needs to their husbands or partners. They must say: this is the way I need you to love me, for it is a requirement for you to love me and also serve me just as I serve you. It is important to start to communicate your needs and to teach the man how you like being loved. This is 100% essential to a happy relationship". You have to read this book to get to know her recommended time-honoured ways to effect and continue to optimise the communication described above.

To the men she gives the advice: "Both of you need to show love every day. Tell your partner that you love being with them. Men, show you love your wife by giving them flowers. Relationships die from complacency. Talk to your partner about ways in which both of you can show love every day". No man would want to miss out on the ways to show love daily hence you need to get this book.

Valerie Muzelenga is right when she states, "Something has gone wrong and we need to fix it together and I believe that little by little we will. We will because it's vital to our happiness".

She demonstrates within this book how we need to go back into our past rich heritage as Africans, irrespective of which of the 54 states on the continent from which we come and to identify many of the positive concepts from our heritage we can employ in the now, to solve present challenges while building and healing fragmented relationships and families as we plot our future.

I commend this lady for her continued stance on what I have over the years called "Cultural integration" which represents sieving and keeping the positive aspects of one culture and merging it with the positive aspects of another while discarding the non progressive negative aspects of both.

Having read this book line by line, I can confidently recommend it as a life manual. It is important to get a copy for one to understand how to generate commendable positive intercultural dialogue across communities and overcome challenges in living and loving.

On a final note, it will be very unfair and not in the spirit of giving to read *The New Way for African Relationships* and not share the book with another person. So, as I wish you a happy and enlightening reading session, I ender you to recommend this life, living and loving manual to those dear to you that they too can share in the joys, knowledge and solutions this book has given you.

LORETTA OGBORO-OKOR
(MRCOG, MBBS, MSc, MSc.Clin.Ed.)

ACKNOWLEDGEMENTS

Mr. and Mrs. Paison Mbewe (My Parents): Thank you For teaching me my Heritage and culture and Values. The skills that have seen me through life. Thank you for your entrepreneurial skills which you passed on without knowing.

To my husband Nixon Muzelenga, for believing in me and giving me the freedom to do what I want without restrictions. For being there in the background and cheering me on.

Mrs. Nancy Tembo: Thank you for the hard work you took on looking after us when dad passed away. You showed us compassion and generosity even as you had to look after your own family. You made sure we all got an Education just as our parents had wanted and we are all empowered and self-reliant.

Mr. Samuel Mbewe: Thank you for being a good brother father and leader of the Mbewe Clan. You are always there for everyone when they are going through a difficult time. You gave us your time, Love, support, and Companionship be it night or day. You took up this Role at a tender age in your teenage years and had to grow up fast.

Nicholas Tembo: For inspiring me to grow and be what I can be. Thank you for putting the spark in my heart, to desire more and work on my personal development, through that small book, Jonathan Livingstone Seagull, by Richard Bach. I started learning how to fly.

My Ancestors and ForeFathers: Thank for letting me stand on your shoulders. Your teachings will continue going a long way.

My Cousins Mrs. Mary Chonta and Mrs. Mushipi: Thank you for sharing the knowledge and embracing our Heritage and dedication to empowering women through marriage Counselling. Our parents played a big part in the community through the services of playing midwives and marriage counsellors.

Mrs. Margaret Chisanga and Christina Shihlomule. My very supportive friends. Thank you for believing in me for supporting me and encouraging me to go for what I want. For putting up with my impulse to continue working instead of joining in the conversation at times.

My Beautiful Coach Ava Eagle Brown for her time, support and holding my hand.

Kaylia Dunstan, My Editor: Thank you for your dedication, time and support.

TABLE OF CONTENTS

INTRODUCTION

WHY I WROTE THIS BOOK

———————

I wrote this book to share the knowledge I learnt from my grandmother, my parents, extended family and the women in the community I grew up in. I've been coming to the realisation over many years that my culture was very rich in many ways and that colonisation, technology and other cultures and beliefs have changed the way my ancestors lived beyond recognition.

My people lived in unity and harmony. Everyone knew each other by name and deeds. The divorce rate was very low if at all. Children listened to their parents and were obedient. When I look around these days, it appears to be a struggle to bring children up well. In many cases, parents have no teeth to properly discipline their children.

The New Way for African Relationships by *Valerie Muzelenga*

Courting and marriage have changed. People have now taken to internet dating sites to find a mate. Men appear to be afraid to talk to women face to face and that skill is dying out little by little.

On the other hand, there is an increase in parents and couples wanting to embrace traditional marriage to help cement their relationships and ensure stable blissful long lasting marriages.

There's a growing need for tradition and knowledge of the old ways to help us to navigate this very confusing world of mixed messages. I wanted to share my story and the traditions of our ancestors to shed light on what has worked for thousands of years.

I remember a time when our children were safer and played outside without any fear of danger. We played outdoor games like hopscotch, jumping rope, hide and seek and rounders. We practiced backflips on piles of fresh cut grass heaped together and many more physical games. There was no obesity. We went to the river to get special clay or mud to make dolls to play with. The boys made toys from wire. We had so many adventures without the knowledge of the parents. We used to tell them we were going to collect firewood. We made TV from cardboard boxes and made cuttings from magazines and newspapers and turned them into characters.

I don't believe that a life of freedom and creativity for children or adults is something of the past. As a counsellor and a member of the community I've seen families struggle, couples on the verge of divorce and children go down the wrong paths. Couples are coming to me saying that their marriage has lost its sparkle and has become dull and boring and they are looking for new ways to make their marriages strong.

Our African tradition had good teachings that made couples stay together till death do them part. There were also parts of the traditions that were not supportive of women including polygamy and women being treated like property by men and diminishing their voices.

This book takes the best of African tradition and also speaks to some of the problems arising because of the fusion of culture. My experience is that couples that are taking the best of our past, including practicing good values are seeing their relationships improve immeasurably. The west also has value and some of the values inherent in Christianity can also be excellent for stable marriages and parenting.

I wrote this book to draw the best from both Africa and the west to educate those who have lost their way in the merging of cultures and to give them hope for themselves, their families, their children and their community.

CHAPTER 1

SOMETHING HAS GONE WRONG AND WE NEED TO FIX IT

———————

"If you want to go quickly, go alone. If you want to go far, go together."
African proverb

Every night when I was a young girl in Zambia, we would spend our evenings by the bonfire. Mum and Dad and our relatives and elders would tell traditional stories that were often filled with meaning and wisdom. We didn't know it at the time but these times by the bonfire were part of our education. The stories taught us about life and living, our parents knew they had the responsibility to teach us how to survive and how to live with dignity and grace. These stories were our history class and family tree lessons.

The bonfire was not the only time we were taught. There were traditions that ensured that our families and elders were alongside us during our youth and as we grew into adulthood. We were taught practical ways to survive and thrive as well as how to treat our elders and our equals.

What we were taught had tremendous value but this is being lost.

ACKNOWLEDGING THE LOSS OF OUR CULTURE

Colonisation brought great change to our Zambian culture. The British Empire was attracted by rich copper and other minerals and decided to colonise Zambia in the early 1900s. David Livingston and other missionaries brought the bible and westernised religion to our land.

Zambians were told that their way of living was backward and not in line with the bible. People were baptised with new English names or those from bible characters. My family kept their traditional ways but some Zambians stopped practicing their traditions and embraced the white man's way of living.

This change was replicated all over Africa, in the places that were colonised.

Suburbs and urban areas sprang up and the rural areas were left behind. There was no electricity in rural areas, only kerosene lamps and cooking using fires. Development in rural areas was limited to a Boma, an office for collecting taxes from the citizens

The British version of civic organisation began to take over. Our people were told they needed to get jobs in the urban areas where the industries were set up. This eroded the rich heritage of our people and disrupted our close unity and way of life and living. Slowly but surely many people of Zambia forgot their traditional practices.

For a while, there were community activities that happened on weekends where the communities consisting of the eight major languages of Zambia would gather and share their traditions including traditional dances, food, and entertainment. This included the NguleWamukulu from the Chewa people in Eastern part of Zambia, the Makishi dance by the Luvales from Northwestern part of Zambia and Akalela and the Infunkutu by the Bemba's from Northern Zambia to mention a few. But over the years, this practice stopped altogether and only remained in schools to showcase on the day of Zambian independence and yearly celebrations of cultural heritage of the eight major languages.

THE NEW WAY

When the white man came they considered us backward and yes, I'm the first to acknowledge that there were aspects of our culture that are better left in the past but in many ways their perception was wrong. There were elements of our culture that were incredibly valuable in fostering happy people and a strong cohesive community. I was lucky that my parents and elders had decided to continue the traditions of our community.

I moved from Zambia to London many years ago and have seen

the effects of the loss of our culture in our African community here and back home.

Gone were the African names, the way of worship and appeasing our ancestors. The dress code and how we looked at things changed dramatically. Parents stopped shepherding their children through the process of our traditions. Family planning was implemented, values changed. Illegitimate children became acceptable in our societies. Divorce went on the increase, which was unheard of before.

We've also seen a fundamental change from value and reverence for the community to value in self above all else. Children have taken on this value and now have permission to demand that they are the centre of the universe instead of understanding that being a respectful part of the community will make them happier as young adults than if they choose to push their individual needs above others.

There are some of us that still uphold the traditional ways and have the wisdom and the knowledge to teach about these ways so that the incredible value of the African culture is not lost.

As a counsellor and elder, my experience is that in the midst of a cultural fragmentation and a deep unhappiness that is arising from the loss of our ways people are now seeking out the old knowledge. They want to know how to embrace the valuable aspects of their culture for themselves and their families. They want to be able to sit down at a symbolic campfire and learn. They want our community back and they especially want their children to know the stories and the wisdom so that they won't fall into deep unhappiness and pain that often results from loss of place and loss of direction.

This book is about mapping out how the African people can embrace their past and their future, how they can integrate African culture into their western existence. It's a book about building strong and powerful relationships and marriages. It's also for the women and men who have fallen in love with an African and who want to also embrace and respect the culture that they are marrying into.

Something has gone wrong and we need to fix it together and I believe that little by little we will. We will because it's vital to our happiness.

CHAPTER 2

THE AFRICAN BLUEPRINT - FINDING VALUE IN OUR PAST

———————

"Don't tear down a fence unless you know why it was put up."
African proverb

"An awareness of our past is essential to the establishment of our personality and our identity as Africans."
Haile Selassie

Colonisation tore down the fence of our culture without knowing why certain traditions worked so well in building harmony, self-respect, self-esteem, respect for others, and a sense of place, happiness, contribution, and boundaries. Our community ties were very strong and help was always at hand when we went through big pain such as sickness or death.

This chapter will outline the cultural traditions that have been proven to have a positive impact on African relationships and people. In many of our communities, this is now called the African blueprint. There are details of the traditions that I can't reveal due to the fact that these are revealed within the secret boundaries of culture but I will outline as much as I can.

The rites of passage were fundamentally important in our culture to provide time-proven clear definition and instruction so that a person knew exactly where they were in their journey and the requirements for their behaviour and actions. They were fundamental to their sense of identity and such a valuable guide.

Although some aspects of the blueprint could be viewed as non-progressive or even sexist these clear definitions provided a sense of place and position within the community. I will go further into how these can be adapted to living in a western culture in subsequent chapters. My advice is to reflect on these traditions building a strong culture and community and reserve your judgements until you've read through the subsequent chapters and have fully comprehended the new way.

> *"Rites of passage play a central role in African socialisation, demarking the different stages in an individual's development, as well as that person's relationship and role in the broader community."*
> **Alik Shadadah**

THE JOY OF BIRTH

"You cannot name a child that is not born."
African proverb

Birth is seen as a celebration in our culture, it confirms that the tribe and/ or community will live on and that social ties will continue to strengthen. The naming of the child is very important and often doesn't happen until it is confirmed that the child is healthy. Often the elders and appropriate community members meet with the parents or engage in ritual or prayer to bless the child with prosperity and a healthy life. The elders often give the name for the child after much contemplation.

A midwife or midwives in the community who are well practiced often take the mother through the process of birthing the child.

Following the birth, the mother is surrounded by her mother and aunties and supported through the overwhelming period of becoming familiar with her child.

The mother's mother and aunties would have spent a long time educating the mother about childbirth and childrearing so that she is fully prepared.

THE POWER OF STORIES THROUGHOUT CHILDHOOD

In the old way, an African child benefited from the teachings of the elders and the senior members of their family as they grew up. Most of the teachings were given in an informal setting such as around the bonfire and children were often told as stories or parables with hidden meanings.

The African culture believed strongly in the power of story to influence and shape behaviour. Through these stories children were told to share things, to love and support one another and their community, to be truthful and to be kind. They featured stories of African animals such as jackals, warthogs, lions and hyenas and also explained why they took the size and shape they did while also imparting lessons.

The children would sit around the bonfires, the campfires, and the community gatherings and learn and the elders gave their time to weave tales and impart knowledge.

The elders and the community were also very persistent about ensuring that the children had respect for their elders and their aunties, uncles, and parents. Respect was often shown through acts of humility such as the child kneeling down when the parent or elders summoned him or her and bringing the hands together when receiving anything from the elders or parents.

The community reinforced this behaviour. If the child acted up then it was not only the responsibility of the parent to reinforce better behaviour, the child would also have to answer to the community. Because the rules for behaviour were so strongly defined the child had a better idea of what was right or what was wrong. That didn't mean that the children were kept overly controlled, they ran free and had adventures and sometimes got into fights. They were children but they also understood more clearly the boundaries for proper behaviour and this resulted mostly in a more harmonious community.

ADULTHOOD & INITIATION

The rite of passage into adulthood was taken very seriously in many of the African tribes. It wasn't seen as simply an event with no preparation and no follow up and it certainly wasn't just passed by, as is commonly the case in western culture.

Adulthood meant responsibility and knowledge and the preparation for adulthood was a long period of teaching adult skills and identities such as problem-solving, appropriate behaviour for men and women, social responsibility, the rules and taboos of the community and the child's purpose in life. The teaching was to equip them to function as healthy and contributing members of the community.

The foundation rite that marked the transition was an initiation, which happened around puberty. Prior to the initiation ceremony, the young adult was taken away to be taught: the male with the males, and the female with the females.

In the eastern part of Zambia, the girls were put in seclusion with a mentor and mother figure for four weeks. She is taught lessons on personal hygiene, the history of her people, how to interact with the elders respectfully as a woman, preparing for parenthood, the importance of remaining chaste until her marriage day given that a husband will be there to support her and her children, how to cook and do housework and laundry.

The young men were taken to what is called Insaka in Bemba and in Chewa it is called Kumphala, where the soon to be husband was taught how to build a house for his bride, how to hunt, fish, farm, garden and prepare land for the planting season. He was advised that it is paramount to look after his bride and their children and what to expect on the wedding day. In some African cultures, the young man was also tested physically, mentally and intellectually to prove his capability to operate as a man in the community. For example, in the Masai culture young men were asked to watch over community's cattle, participate in cattle raids and kill a lion. In Hamar and Karo societies a young man must run over the backs of twenty to forty cattle.

This preparation was essential for imparting to the young adults how to conduct themselves in marriage, business, and society. It was very much about building strong practical and relationship skills so that the couple would live in harmony with each other and themselves. It was respected that the elders that took them through the period of seclusion knew what they were talking about because this wisdom had been honed for thousands of years.

It must be said that some African societies condoned female circumcision as part of the initiation process. As a nurse I have seen the results of this and how much pain it resulted in for an adult woman trying to birth a child and cannot condone that element of the initiation process. The new way is about taking the good from the culture and moving on from the destructive elements.

The initiation ceremony was held when the young adult was fully prepared. The old was gone and the new would start from that moment on. Initiation could involve physical changes such marks, shaved heads, the burning of the old clothing and also symbolic changes such as a new name. Can you imagine if this happened to western teenagers of today with their overblown concept of their own identity? The initiation was often marked by a reunion of the male or female their family and community and a great celebration.

In the Twa culture, the girl joined other girls in seclusion and then after their teaching was finished they came out dancing and were celebrated with great joy in their community.

MARRIAGE PREPARATION

Marriage was seen as absolutely critical for the sustainability of the community and the culture in Africa. It was an essential part of the journey of a human being and so much was done from an early age to train individuals to be prepared and to honour marriage.

Marriage represented the joining of two families and sometimes two communities and was also about providing the couple with a joint purpose and a strong direction. Forming bonds was essential to African community and this is the paramount symbol of bond forming.

Marriage was also about the continuation of the community through childbirth. That's why people refusing to get married seemed illogical by traditional African communities.

In our community, if there was an indication that a man and a woman were suitable for marriage the man's relative would come to ask for the girl's hand in marriage with a token in the form of money. This acted as an icebreaker before stating the intention of the visit. Often the relative would say that they want the engagement to be official. Marriage negotiations were done and the man is charged with what is called (Lobola), a bride price. This is to symbolise that the man is receiving a gift that he will spend the rest of his life with. Every man is expected to pay the bride price. Usually, the responsibility used to fall on the uncles of the groom and they paid in herds of cows. As people don't rear cows nowadays in towns, the current price of cattle is converted into monetary value.

Marriage preparation was taken very seriously and information taught during the puberty and initiation rites was further expanded on for both men and women including details about sex and procreation. No stone was left unturned and all of their questions were answered.

The marriage ceremony was a happy community affair with

many rituals and gifts imparted during the event. In the old ways, everyone in the community was free to attend rather than sending invitations and limiting attendance. On the day before the wedding women gathered to do the cooking and different dishes were prepared. The community contributed gifts so that the event could be successful. The men would kill a cow or goat for the wedding feast.

The groom was assigned a male mentor called Bashibukombe. This mentor represented the groom and was responsible for the teachings. The bride had a lady mentor called APhungu.The assigned teachers were mandated to check that what was taught was demonstrated by the couple by carrying out certain activities during what is now called the bridal shower. In the old days, this tradition would be an overnight and the elderly married women would gather and teach the bride through songs and dance, ululate, eating and celebrating. Here the women would also showcase their dancing skills.Role playing is also done in different situations.

In the very rural areas, women would be taught to wake up early to go and fetch water from the well or borehole for cooking and bathing. She would look for firewood, sweep the compound yard and heat water for her husband and other family members. However, if she was a lazy bride who spent most of her time doing nothing and left all the housework and day to day running of the home the elders would advise her that there were consequences for her actions such as her husband falling in love with someone else due to lack of care.

The same applied to the man who could lose his new bride to another man if he was lazy and didn't care for her. Laziness was not condoned in African culture, there was too much to be done to survive.

On the marriage night, the designated women escorted the bride to the husband's homestead and the same women woke up early to check on the bride and groom to find out how they spent the first married night together. If there were any problems they were noted and reported back to the parents. Some problems that may have arisen were erectile dysfunction or vaginismuses, which is pain experienced by the bride or woman during penetration due to vaginal muscle spasms. The older men and women knew how to rectify these problems, so help was at hand.

In many African cultures, the marriage is not seen as fully recognised until the woman became pregnant and the elders would do everything possible to help the couple start a family. These days because of Christianity this is practice is not as bad as it was before. Nowadays the stigma of a woman not falling pregnant has reduced.

THE ROLE OF ELDERS

"When an old man dies a library burns to the ground."
African proverb

*"The words of the elders do not lock all the doors;
they leave the right door open."*
Zambian proverb

Elders were essential to African communities. Their primary role was to ensure the young were taught and transition well into adult life and to provide guidance and wisdom to the community as a whole.

Most communities ensured the elders 'physical needs were looked after so that they could have more time to commune with the spiritual and to share the insights they gained with the community. It was seen as a great privilege to have an elder in your home.

There were also strict rules about how an elder should behave and that they should not manipulate or misuse their power for their own ends.

They were the holders of the history and wisdom of the tribe and their job was to pass this on.

The fact that everyone in an African community had access to a source of wisdom, comfort, and guidance was incredibly valuable for the mental and emotional health of the community.

Imagine if you could go to someone who has lived a lot of life and who is open to you and has known you since you were born and you can ask them to help you sort out your thoughts and ask them for their wisdom that is garnered not only from their own life but from the lives of the generations before them, time honoured wisdom passed down and given to you. As a westernised teenager you might not get just how wonderful that would be but as an adult struggling to make sense of a complicated life I know most of you would so appreciate an elder in your midst.

When my grandmother who was an elder died in the village of

District Chadidza the surrounding communities and the one she lived in gathered together. She was the oldest in the village and had no proper birth certificate to verify her age, but she talked about a great war some men had to go and fight in. She passed on in 1990. It was believed she was over a hundred years old. If I remember correctly also she spoke of how they used to run and hide in the bush when the white man came to collect taxes. The funeral gathering was huge and people came from near and far. The village headman made the war cry when it was time to bring grandma's coffin from the house and proceed to the graveyard. The warriors did the war dance and they were dressed in Angoni style Regalia. Some cows were slaughtered and some goats. It turned out to be a celebration of her life and the loss of such an elder in the village.

I learnt a lot from my grandmother in her house at the fireside. No question was too complicated for her to answer. On matters of the heart and love, she had a lot to say. She was mourned with grace and it was an honour the way they sent her off. Her death was the end of a certain generation and era.

DEATH

In many African societies, there is a belief that the spirit of the dead person is still with the living and a part of the community. The death rites are very important in ensuring that the person receives the correct status in their afterlife. Some more notable members of the community such as particularly effective elders can be seen as ancestors to ask guidance of after they have passed.

When a death occurs in the family in urban areas the body is taken to the mortuary if it is in town. The funeral is unique in the sense that it is a mixture of west and Zambian tradition in urban areas. The family members are informed via phone and text messages. A member of the family will be sent to ZNBC Zambia Broadcasting cooperation to put in a notice of the deceased when burial will take place, which cemetery burial will be taking place and which family members the message is for. It's been customary since I was growing up for ZNBC Radio or TV to read out the death announcement, with sombre music playing in the background after each news bulletin.

The women remove furniture from the house in the lounge and put it outside for men to sit on. Women stay in the house and do a lot of mourning. The men go out to buy the casket and make the funeral arrangements. The men take the women to buy foodstuffs from the market or shops. In the eastern part of Zambia, the men's cry goes like thisMai baba-beee Mai baba-beee. The women's cry is known as chitengo and is Ye-ee-eegh.It's a different kind of cry, very distinct with grief. Family members arriving at the funeral house start a cry called Kukhuza soon as they get out of the car at the gate or just as they walk through the gate.

In the rural areas death is announced by sending someone on a bicycle to surrounding villages. A distinct cry also alerts people in the village that there is a death. People gather and enter the house of the host and pass condolences and mourn with them. If they died in the night or early hour's burial takes place on the same day. The responsibility of organising the funeral proceedings is left to the men. The community help by contributing an African mealie meal and other foodstuffs. The women do the cooking to feed the mourners.

After burial in all instances, they carry out a ritual called Kupywera, which is sweeping the house and the yard.

Death is a taboo subject. Even when I was growing up my parents did not discuss death and dying with us children. I've written about my fear of dead bodies and how I overcame this in the anthology, The Journey to Purpose, which is available for sale on my website - www. valeriecounselling.com

Immediately after burial or the following day, a family meeting was held and the family would discuss who would look after children. They also chose an administrator of the estate and distribution of property. Those relatives who wished to have their hair cutdidso. The younger members of the family would have a small strand of hair cut from the back of their head. Those who were married were given secret instructions in keeping with the traditions. The wife was instructed to wear a black dress for a year. The wife's head was shaved and a black headscarf was worn. If a man remained after the death of his wife they put a black armband on his upper arm. This was for identification in the community that he or she had lost a spouse.

At the end of that year, the community would brew traditional beer to appease the ancestors and also put a tombstone or cement on the grave of the deceased. The practice now depends on the age of the remaining partner and also logistics for those traveling from the village. All processes are done in one day so that the cost of travel expenses is reduced.

If a spouse died the elders chose a relative from either side to take the name of the deceased. If a woman died a female relative took the name if a man died a male relative took the name. This person became the father head or mother head for the children and ensured that the children weren't left out of the community or treated as orphans. They made certain that the children got an education and were provided for by liaising with the chosen administrator to provide funds. If the remaining spouse is able to look after his or her children they do so. Family representative takes over only if they are financially challenged.

The widow or widower would sit on a reed mat called Mphasa. A chosen child or older person smeared white corn meal on their forehead and jumped or stepped over their legs. This was done to signify that the widow or widower was free to remarry if they wished and to comfort them that the deceased would not haunt them.

It is quite common in African communities for those who have died to enter the dreams of the living. A Luo man, for example, could not sleep with another woman until he has dreamed of having sex with his wife.

Bad events in a community can also be seen as a sign that the ancestors are angry or unhappy with the community. The way to make this right is for the people and the community to follow ethical behaviour and to do right by others. Death in this way provides an ethical policing of community standards and is also a vital reminder that physical life is short and that good behaviour will be honoured in the afterlife.

The Christian communities replicate the idea of life after death although in many cases Christians see the dead as going to heaven and not present on earth. It is the belief in some African/Christian communities that the dead sleep in the graves waiting for the second coming of Jesus Christ drawing on the bible verse, "The Lord himself shall descend from heaven with a shout, with the voice of the archangel, and with the trump of God: and the dead in Christ will rise first." 1Thessalonians 4:16-17.

This sense of continuation is similar and can be drawn upon when attempting to pave a new way forward for present African relationships.

THE RIGHT TO IMPART WISDOM AND GUIDANCE

In many African cultures, you could not express your opinion and try to direct the views of the tribe unless you could show that you were properly trained to speak about such matters.

This mirrors the tradition of the Christian churches and many other religions and traditional social structures.

This ensured that influencing opinions were made by those with the knowledge and the experience to make them rather than just anyone putting forward random ideas based on loosely held beliefs.

This right to impart wisdom and guidance ensured that the community went in a solid and well-founded direction instead of making unwise decisions and fragmenting because of the vast number of opinions being made. This tradition was also upheld through rituals and practices of respect.

The logic of this becomes obvious when we look at the growth of social media and the rise of unwise and uneducated opinions influencing communities and the world and wreaking havoc and destruction. It's also a further example of the rise of individualism and the lack of respect for education and scholarship.

CHAPTER 3

THE NEW WAY FOR AFRICAN ROMANCE AND MARRIAGE

"Where there is love there is no darkness."
Burundi

*"Love is patient, love is kind. It does not envy, it does not boast, it is not proud.
It does not dishonour others, it is not self-seeking, it is not easily angered, and it
keeps no record of wrongs. Love does not delight in evil but rejoices with the truth.
It always protects, always trusts always hope, and always perseveres."*
1 Corinthians 13:4-7

As a marriage and relationship counsellor, I get an inside view on the
current state of relationships. I counsel African, Black and multiracial
couples who are either preparing for marriage or going through marriage
difficulties. I also counsel women who want to bring more fire, love, and

enjoyment into their relationships. There are a number of themes that come up during counselling that are arising across the board and can be attributed to the stresses and patterns of living of modern societies and also the loss of culture and identity that I talked about in the last chapter. I'm going to address each of these themes and give you some counselling via this book as to how you can address these in your romantic relationships. I'll draw upon the best of African and western culture and give you a new way including new insights into how to build amazing and fulfilling marriages.

WE MISUNDERSTAND EACH OTHER

In the old traditions, years were spent teaching young men and women how they should behave, what the accepted behaviours are and their roles within the marriage and relationship. Nowadays many urbanised Africans in Africa and overseas don't receive any of this training. Because there's no guide there's also a great element of navigating blindly and a great capacity for misunderstanding.

I see this all the time during counselling. Couples are constantly misunderstanding each other and because of this, they decide to divorce. This then causes further pain for them and for their children if they have any.

But there's another way, that draws on both African and western traditions. The basis for misunderstanding is that you don't get the other person's perspective. Maybe they have grown up differently to you; maybe they have different values and beliefs. The role for both the male and the female in the relationship is to understand each other. Both people need to put aside their egos and start to see life through the other person's eyes. In essence, you are starting the process that started very young in African culture; you are educating yourself. This must be done deliberately and with love. I give couples the following exercise to start this process off and encourage them to build this into their marriage.

★ HOT ISSUE EXERCISE

Every two weeks I want you to set aside some time in the evening with your partner just for you. Make sure there are no distractions. Bring with you two exercise books and/or something that you can write in. Then I want you to:

1. Choose a topic that's been a hot or difficult issue for you. Maybe it's something to do with how you treat each other, your children, the way the house is managed. It needs to be something that's causing disagreements that haven't been sorted.

2. Then each of you writes down how you view the issue, how it makes you feel and the things that you can do to make the situation better. Do this for about 10-15 minutes.

3. Exchange your books and read what the other person has written and make sure you have the attitude of wanting to understand them and see their perspective.
4. Then sit facing each other and look each other in the eyes with your knees touching.
5. Discuss what you've read for 10 minutes, no longer, then state very clearly what each of you is going to do better.

This exercise gets right to the heart of misunderstandings and helps to build stronger perspectives. Each person must start to learn that they are not always right but what is more important is that they understand each other and that there's a clear way forward for the issue with steps that need to be taken to make things better. So often we argue about hot issues but we never really address them outside of the argument where we feel passionate and angry. At first, this exercise will feel foreign and uncomfortable but if it becomes a practice the misunderstanding will reduce, as you'll understand each other more overall.

MISUNDERSTANDING LOVE

Western culture has told us for years that we must seek love above all else in relationships and that this will sustain us.

Love is a feeling based on chemical attraction and sometimes a possible synchronicity between two people's minds and values. When people fall in love they are experiencing a chemical reaction in their bodies and this gives them feelings of happiness and excitement.

The problem with seeing this kind of hyper Hollywood romantic love as the foundation for a relationship is that the chemical reaction that happens will die away and then couples are left to try to handle what is left. Those who are extremely sexually attracted to each other but don't have personalities, values, and history that blend well together often have the worst types of relationships as there's only conflict when the sexual attraction eventually fades.

When I was growing up in Zambia we had the capacity to associate with other boys and when it got to the point where they were interested in us, we would consult with the senior members of our family who would then consult with the other family and look at formal introductions. Some might see this as interference from the family but it was the family's job to make sure that we were a suitable match and that the young man had the qualities that would work well within the community.

There was still the idea of love but it always worked alongside compatibility. It was incredibly important that the two people were compatible.

As western culture has swallowed the idea of just the feeling of love as being the thing that makes people get married and have a wonderful life together it's important that we reframe this and present relationships as both the feeling of love but also a focus on compatibility.

Trust me that as the years roll on your compatibility will make your life happier as you'll have similar values, compatible interests and see life in similar ways. Your differences, as you are bound to have differences, as well as partnerships, are never perfect, will then seem less overwhelming.

I've provided two practices for you below. The first will focus on those of you that are single and looking for relationships and the second will be for those of you that are in a relationship and want to make it better.

★ LOOKING FOR LOVE PRACTICE – ASKING THE RIGHT QUESTIONS

"Marriage is like a groundnut; you have to crack them to see what is inside"
Ghanaian proverb

From now on when you are actively seeking love and relationships seek people that you are attracted to of course but this time spend some time getting to know them before you engage in any sexual practice. I encourage the Christians I counsel to wait till marriage but if you can't wait then set a time period before you have sex.

The reason for this is very important. This will give you the ability to really understand whether you are truly compatible with your potential partner in life. Remember that after the chemicals die down you will have years of being with this person so you will need to really like being with them and if you have similar values and interests then this will make things a whole lot easier.

Also, it's important to note that if you like someone you are more likely to want to engage sexually with them years down the track. So when you meet a potential mate see if you can find out the following about them and then discuss with wise friends and elders around you whether there's compatibility there.

- What things does your potential partner value? Do they value wealth over love? Do they value family? Do they value their friends more than you? Do they value working hard or not working hard?

- What values do they have? Love? Greed? Power? Kindness? Care for those who are struggling? Honour? Truth?

- What are their interests? Could you see yourself doing similar things or supporting these interests? Are his or her interests something that doesn't interest you at all and could even repel you?

- Do they have a similar upbringing? What was different about their upbringing to yours and is that having a positive or negative influence on their present behaviour? Are you ok with this for the rest of your life?

- Make sure you spend time with your partner in different situations. See how they react and what they do. Make sure that you spend time doing what you want to do as much as what he or she wants to do. See if they are controlling or easy going or fun loving or kind.

- If there are differences in your upbringing or your traditions is your potential partner enthusiastic about understanding these differences? Are you enthusiastic about understanding theirs?

The above may sound like I'm asking you to give them a job interview but just remember that this is a person you are going to have to spend a long time with and the more compatible you are the happier you will be. You are not looking for perfection but you are looking for someone that will compliment you and be kind to you and value the same things as you do. As per the tradition of our ancestors find someone who is going to fit in your tribe.

★ FOSTERING COMPATIBILITY IN YOUR RELATIONSHIP EXERCISE

If you find yourself in a relationship that may not be greatly compatible you have the choice to leave or to work on the relationship. Remember that if you decide to leave you may be inheriting another set of big problems with a new partner depending on how strongly you interrogate your compatibility when you first start seeing each other.

If you choose to start working on compatibility you must be very focused, as you'll be breaking ingrained relationship patterns that have developed over the time you've been together.

The first thing I want you to do is to set some time aside with each other and sit down with a piece of paper and work out where your similarities are. I call this a similarity brainstorm. Write down everything you agree on and every activity that you approach in a similar way and like doing together. I want you to discuss these similarities and find happiness from realising that there are some things that you both like doing.

Now I want you to look at this brainstorm and I want you to both think of one thing that you really want to do as individuals and would like your partner to do also. It might be going for a bike ride, dancing, going to a big sports game or taking your kids to a show.

And I want you both to agree to do the one thing that you want to do because it will draw you closer together as you'll have shared experiences and you'll be increasing your compatibility. Often these things we desire are closely linked to our values as well so there's a chance that by agreeing to do each other's activities you are coming closer together in terms of what you value.

You are agreeing to build community within your family unit. You must also both agree to have a positive attitude when you do this activity and you may not do it again but there's a chance that you'll like it.

Building compatibility is always about building positive experiences that increase your desire to be with each other.

CONFUSION OVER DOMINANCE AND SUBMISSION – COMMUNICATING YOUR NEEDS

"African women, in general, need to know that it's OK for them to be the way they are - to see the way they are as a strength, and to be liberated from fear and from silence."
Wangari Maathai

One of the aspects of African culture that's contentious from the perspective of the west is the emphasis on the dominance of males and the submission of females. In many African cultures, people are taught that the women are weaker and that the men should rule the household. This has resulted in some issues for the human rights of women, domestic abuse and even reports that women are taught that they should see a man hitting them as a sign of love.

The Christian religion has also taught for centuries that wives should submit to their husbands quoting the bible verse:

"Wives submit to your husband's as to the Lord."
Ephesians 5:22

My experience is that unhealthy submission, where the women completely submit to the men leads to unhappy marriages, as the woman is given no value. As the writer, Alice Walker says, "No person is your friend who demands your silence, or denies your right to grow."

In Zambia, women are starting to gain positions of power and are establishing themselves as professionals but still in some quarters the emphasis is that they should submit completely to a man.

What was no emphasised in the past in Christian religion and in some African traditions was that if the woman submits to the man the man must love and adore the woman and support her completely, which is another form of submission but it's submission of love and adoration. As Ephesians 5:25 says, "Husbands love your wives just as Christ loved the church and gave himself up for her."

The emphasis in traditional African communities was very much on ensuring harmony within the tribe. Harmony cannot happen when one person is suppressed by another. It is not the way to happiness. Only true love, which is the love that serves and adores through thick and thin from both sides is the way to ensure a happy relationship. As the Burundi proverb says, "Where there is love there is no darkness."

How can women then ensure that they are not in a place of submission? It is essential that they communicate their needs to their husbands or partners. They must say: this is the way I need you to love me, for it is a requirement for you to love me and also serve me just as I serve you.

I've found through years of counselling that some African women, in particular, find it difficult to speak their needs clearly and then get upset when the man just does what he wants. This lack of ability to communicate needs may come from years of training in submission or it just may be personality. Regardless, it's important to start to communicate your needs and to teach the man how you like being loved. This is 100% essential to a happy relationship. Here are some time-honoured ways to do this.

★ TIPS FOR COMMUNICATING YOUR LOVE NEEDS AS A WOMAN

For women, in particular, it's very important to start to become aware of your physical needs as this is one of the key parts of your relationship that will need fostering.

When you are alone, carry out an assessment of your body to become familiar with it and know which part of your body gives you tingling sensations.

When you find these erogenous zones you should share this information with your husband. For example, "If you touch and play with my nipples I feel turned on. If you caress my inner thigh and touch me on the skin I feel good. I like this way of kissing."

Direct him or her with your hands where you want to be touched and demonstrate how fast or slow stroke.

Be honest. It's only when you tell him that he will know what to do with you. Some men think a 10-second kiss or peck on the cheek counts as foreplay. Show him or direct his hands to the treasure trough, the clitoris. This small organ with multiple nerve endings is there for the pleasure of the woman.

For a very long time, men thought that sex is for pleasure for them and procreation only for a woman. No, it is not.

Women are waking up from this slumber that sex means much

more. Women are beginning to know the journey they must take to experience the Big O orgasm.

The G-spot is another place of pleasure for a woman. This is presumed to be about 50-80mm inside the vagina, on the front wall. Show the man the G-spot and how to get it. For some women playing with this area brings about more intense orgasm, than clitoral. A liquid like urine can be released which is female ejaculation or squirting.

Your needs are also related to what happens outside of the bedroom. Make sure that you tell your husband that he should treat you with respect to and no put-downs in front of friends and relatives   .

He should shower you with love, adoration, and loyalty and be able to make sacrifices when needed like giving up a night with the boys if you are sick and helping around the house if needed. Your husband has equal responsibility for the relationship and should devote time to you.

Have a dialogue with your man and speak with love. Do not attack or accuse but say how you feel when something happens and needs to be corrected. Let the man be a man and treat him with respect and humility. Choose a time when both of you are not stressed. I recommend the early hours of the morning around 4-5am. By this time the children are asleep if you have kids. There must be no shouting or screaming. Show mutual respect.

After 10 mins and you feel you have not been heard it's time to take time out and you can schedule another time to resolve whatever is wrong.

THE PASSION IN THE BEDROOM IS GONE

One of the outcomes of in imbalance in dominance and submission is a very unsatisfactory sex life. A man may have been taught that a woman is a vessel for his needs or simply may be lazy in bed. A woman may not know how to communicate her needs and therefore the man never really knows what she wants.

Good sex is very important in a marriage or relationship to cement physical ties between couples. This issue has become so important that I conduct seminars, counselling and training for women to bring back the fire into their bedrooms, see my website for more details: www.valeriecounselling.com

The number one rule for women in the bedroom is to tell the man what they want. The number one rule for men is to forget about themselves and learn more about how they can serve the goddess aspect of the woman. As I already provide in-depth advice for women in my seminars, a little of which has been shared in the previous section, I'll give you some advice for the men, as a happy wife means a happy life.

★ TIPS FOR MEN IN THE BEDROOM

- Sex starts in the morning. During the day send love and saucy messages as this lets the other person know you are thinking of them.

- Take a shower together and be imaginative or have a bubble bath together. This keeps you connected and reduces the amount of heating up needed to be ready for the act.

- Sharing an apple with your partner is a great way to get rid of halitosis (bad breath) and carry on kissing.

- Caressing the skin with a silky scarf, or tie or small feather duster tantalises the skin to respond sexually. I know others feel ticklish and want to laugh it out.

- Use honey, smear it on the most sensitive part and lap it up.

- Sex is not just about penetration. It's about the relationship between the two of you and the joining of your souls.

- A woman must be warmed up to sex. The more you warm her through touch during the day and leading up to the event the more she's going to give back and enjoy sex. Sexual verbal play is also a great way to warm her up and doing things for her during the day such as cooking her dinner help to make her feel loved and ready for sex.

- Ask the woman to show you the parts that excite her fast when you touch caress her.

- Personal hygiene is important here, no smelly feet, armpits and bad breath as they kill the passion.

- Shave the private parts especially if you practice going down there.

Strawberry hair is a no go zone.

- Ensure you have a towel or incontinent sheets and user-friendly wipes for aftercare.

- Ask your partner how you can serve them and let them explain. Not every woman wants the fast and furious, be slow and gentle and tender.

- Whisper sweet nothings in her ear, you can speak dirty if it is acceptable in your relationship.

- Use your imagination and vary the style of play, positions and discuss what else you want to bring to the table including sex toys. Some African men find this a challenge to their manhood and look down on the use of toys to spice up the romance, but that is not the case at all, it's about pleasure. Women are now demanding more in terms of pleasure.

MOTHERING THE MAN

One of the big complaints of people I counsel is that the women in relationships often find they are mothering their men. Given that the male identity has been eroded from the tradition and many men aren't taught how to provide for their women and take responsibility for the household what's left are men who are looking for their mothers to take care of them.

Some of you may have liked a man who appeared to take

responsibility and they started to show dependency after marriage, given that the common elements of home life meant that he fell into the same pattern of wanting to be looked after by the woman in the house.

This is almost the opposite of the problem of men being overly dominant in a house although often men want to be looked after but also want to call the shots which makes them twice as difficult to live with.

Sadly, many women find themselves having to leave the man because the practice is so ingrained and they become completely drained with the man refusing to contribute to the woman's emotional and physical welfare.

We have the ability as women to ensure this type of pattern doesn't happen with our sons and they are taught responsibility and skills from an early age. Giving young boys household tasks and teaching them how to fix things is a good way of making them more responsible and more able.

It really comes down to the woman clearly articulating her needs and the man deciding whether he's going to step up or not.

The one thing the woman must not do is continue to pander to the man as a mother. The true testament to whether a man will step up is to take away the traditional elements of mothering such as constant servitude. If a man decides not to step up and take responsibility then he must reap the consequences of his actions. Remember that men were warriors. That they had to hunt for the food, provide and protect their families. The way we can teach them to be warriors is to make sure we do not continue to treat them as sons.

A man should also actively seek training and counselling on how to rediscover his warrior if it is lost. The warrior and protector can also be loving and kind, not violent and oppressive.

FINDING A GOOD MAN

Many women come to me and say that they cannot find a good man. The loss of tradition has in some cases resulted in the loss of male responsibility and a clear understanding of loving leadership. It is unfortunate that good men are hard to find but they are around.

Remember not to be caught up in western Hollywood ideals of love but to look for a man that you are attracted to and are also compatible with.

Look for someone with honour and integrity but don't put boundaries around your search. Look for the men that aren't the centre of attention. Remember the Sudanese proverb, "A large chair does not make a king." Find the ones that have worked on themselves.

In Africa, our tribes would go searching for food and water to sustain them. Overcome your fears and put yourself in new situations, meeting new people and know that the universe operates in mysterious ways.

If you are a Christian or religious pray for the man of honour to come into your life but don't sit back and wait, get active.

Regardless of the outcome you will know that you've been as proactive as possible and that you've looked for compatibility and connection rather than superficial attraction. I find this African proverb beautiful as it speaks of the true joy of a healthy relationship - "Between true friends even water drunk together is sweet enough."

You want someone who will love doing the simple things with you, who want to work on the relationship with you and who is a true and gentle king.

CHAPTER 4

LOVE TIPS
WAYS TO INJECT MORE LOVE, MORE STABILITY, MORE COMMUNICATION AND MORE EXCITEMENT INTO YOUR RELATIONSHIPS OR YOUR MARRIAGE

———————

Couples and individuals come to me all the time asking for tips to improve their love lives and their marriages. In the last chapter, I gave you some pointers as to how to improve the issues in your marriage. This chapter is all about building on the positivity and finding a new way forward that makes you both happy.

WALK YOUR OWN PATH

Your love is unique, it's gifted to you and it's amazing that you both found each other and are now living life together. In the same way, you need to build your relationship with your own rules and make your decisions on what is the best for the both of you. Other family members and friends may judge you for what you've decided to do and how you navigate your relationship but if it's working for you then that's what matters. Draw from your heritage and walk your own path. Protect the love you have and decide how you are going to inspire it and keep it aflame.

PLAN TOGETHER

Marriage is a partnership and it's vitally important that you plan the important life decisions together. I recommend you both talk about what you can do to contribute to life growth that draws upon your strengths rather than one person allocate roles and responsibilities. If one is better at booking holidays then let them do this, if the other is better at organising transport let them do this. Play on your strengths.

IMPROVE YOUR COMMUNICATION

I gave you the hot issues exercise in the last chapter to help to kick-start improvements in your communication with each other but this is just the start. It's important to start to look at how you both communicate on a daily basis. Here are some tips to vastly improve your communication.

Be honest

Always try to be as honest as you can with your partner as honesty means that there's nothing eating away underneath and everything is on the table. That said, if you are a perfectionist or judgemental take a look at yourself first and work through whether your issue has arisen because you want to take your partner down a rung or pick them up on something because they don't meet your ideals.

Watch your body language

What body language do you use when you are communicating with your partner? Is it open and respectful or closed and disrespectful? How can you work on your body language to show the other person that you are open and receptive to what they have to say?

Summarise your partner's words

Work on trying to understand what the other person is saying and then summarise it back to them in a loving way. Ask them if your summary is correct and how they would change it. When you summarise what they have to say you are automatically trying to understand their viewpoint.

Work on your tone

How can you use tone to help to convey your message? Is your tone gentle and loving or disrespectful and angry? Can you work on improving your tone so that the other person doesn't get defensive? Ask your partner to give you feedback on your tone so you know what tone works for them so that they are receptive to your message.

Choose the right time and do it face-to-face

Make sure you are mindful of the right time to bring up issues. For example, it's not wise to bring up issues when you are trying to get the kids out the door or via text. Try to be patient and find a time that hasn't got so many distractions.

Foster positive communication habits

Above all foster positive communication. Tell each other the things you appreciate about each other. Start to see each other's quirks as more a part of a wonderful whole and not something to be demeaned. Remember no one is perfect so we are bound to make mistakes. Decide whether it's better to forgive. Compliment and do things for each other that show communication through action.

KEEP YOUR BELIEFS AT THE CENTRE

My husband and I have a deep belief in Jesus Christ and are dedicated Christians. We also have a passion for honouring the best of the African traditions and keeping our communities alive and thriving. If you have core beliefs keep them at the centre of your marriage. Make sure that you honour and give time to them and engage in communities that share the same beliefs.

At the centre of the Christian belief is the doctrine of love, to love one another. This value lies at the centre of my relationship with my husband under Christ and ensures that we show respect, love, and kindness to each other. Because we both regularly go to church we are reminded of our purpose to love others and this keeps us on track.

Whatever your core beliefs are, make sure that you foster these and be vigilant about praying and communicating about your beliefs with your partner.

YOU ARE NOT ALWAYS RIGHT

If you are to succeed in any relationship you must understand and be able to work with the fact that you are not always right. When we come into any discussion we have our own viewpoint based on our history, our past relationships, our experiences and our personality and we think that our viewpoint is valid.

Sometimes it's not, sometimes the other person is making more sense and sometimes you are both wrong. We must develop the ability to see value in what the other person has said. In the same way, you must be able to also understand that you are wrong and be able to acknowledge that to your partner. There are plenty of times in my relationship where we have an argument and I work out that my partner is actually correct. I must be able to say this.

Remember that your ego is there to help you to survive but it must also not destroy things. You must both be of the opinion that two minds are better than one.

ACCEPT IMPERFECTION

Marriages and relationships work when we acknowledge that we are with someone who has good qualities and not so favourable qualities and that in order to make them feel loved we must love the whole.

Statistically, marriages stay together when the partners aren't looking for perfection and are more realistic about the qualities of the person they love.

Sometimes qualities that we perceive as being unfavourable can actually help the relationship and the family. For example, a procrastinator that thinks a lot can come up with great ideas or a person that is too emotional can be the one that reminds everyone that they need to be more human and loving. Regardless, your life will be a lot happier if you accept the good with the bad. You've been fed a solid diet of Hollywood nonsense that tells you that perfection is possible but I'm telling you that imperfection can so often be perfection.

MAKE SURE YOU SHOW LOVE EVERYDAY

Show love every day. Be dedicated to this. Show the one you love that you adore them by being affectionate, by doing lovely things they don't expect. Both of you need to show love every day. Tell your partner that you love being with them. Men, show you love your wife by giving them flowers.

Relationships die from complacency. Talk to your partner about ways in which you can show love every day.

BE GRATEFUL

Relationships can turn corners if both partners focus on what they are grateful for in the relationship and also in each other as individuals. A good way to kick start feeling grateful is to imagine what it would be like if your partner was gone from your life. What would you miss? What positive qualities have you forgotten about? What would life be like without them? Get together and talk about this. Understand that even though life has worn you down there are things in the other person that are beyond valuable.

STEP UP

Both of you need to step up if you want an amazing relationship. You both need to contribute. It's not going to work if only the woman or the man makes the effort. Both must stop taking the relationship for granted and both must agree to fix it.

If one person steps up and the other doesn't then one is becoming a parent and the other a child. One will become dependent on the other. If your partner is lazy then they need to fix this or they will lose you. You must both come to the table and agree to build something better.

PICK YOUR BATTLES

I mentioned timing in my tips above in that you need to choose the right time to bring up issues but if we go deeper than this it's also important to decide whether you are going to accept a quality of your partner that is causing you agitation or not. This may be something that you've fought about before and he or she has said they are going to improve but months later they are back where they started. You must ask yourself whether the quality is truly damaging to the relationship and to your family if you have one or if this quality is simply the person.

Some people are slow movers and they annoy other people who like to move fast, some people like to chill out while others like to keep stimulated, some people are very affectionate, some are mildly affectionate, some people like to organise while others are terrible at it.

Often our partners will make small moves to change their personalities to promote harmony in the relationships but fundamentally they can't be exactly what we want them to be because they are not us. I've talked about accepting imperfection in this chapter and just as importantly you need to decide whether the battle you have is because you want something and don't care what the other person wants or because their behaviour is destroying the relationship. If it's the former, you can decide to accept or not, if it's the later, you can decide whether this is what you want.

IF YOU PRAY, THEN PRAY

Prayer is talking to God, asking for help or an expression of gratitude and thanks. God answers prayers of Christians who ask him or who intercede for others. One needs to have a relationship with God and a connection daily through prayer and supplication.

For a marriage to really work in the Christian setting the couple must have the confidence through the bible, which says "For the eyes of the Lord are on the righteous and his ears are attentive to their prayer."

Marriage was made to be a mirror of God. The bible has a

blueprint too of how couples should behave towards each other. Marriage is holy and couples need the three sides of the triangle to have peace and harmony in their relationship. That is man, wife, and God at the top.

If a couple is having problems in their relationship calling on the name of the lord brings solutions to the problem, but one also has to be silent and learn how God speaks. When there is too much noise it's very easy to miss out on his answers and then we do anything from our own point of view and wonder why we have no peace.

The bible in the book of Song of Solomon talks about love and sex. God talks about how a man and woman should cleave to each other and God ordained marriage in the Garden of Eden. The bible says, "Unless the Lord builds the house, its builders labour in vain." Psalms 127:1.

I believe it's important to pray and take our problems to God so we avoid becoming bitter, unforgiving and unkind. Through prayer, we ask God to help to solve our marriage problems.

CHAPTER 5

A NEW WAY FOR AFRICAN WOMEN

———————

"One of the lessons that I grew up with was to always stay true to yourself and never let what somebody else says distract you from your goals."
Michelle Obama

In this present time, we have an opportunity as black women to truly take hold of our lives and become the women we've always wanted to be. We have a vast heritage that honoured community and relationships about all else and we have the opportunity to draw together as a community in whatever place we live and teach the ways of dignity, self-confidence, and respect and help to empower each other to reach our goals.

The old ways may have dissipated to some extent but we are here to build relationships and community and I believe we're going to do it.

There are some core values we need to really focus on to do this that derive from our heritage and are also the best of modern culture.

If you find you are in relationships, friendships or marriages that do not value the below then it may be time to consider whether these relationships are toxic. As women, we can't move forward if toxic friendships and associations surround us. Moving closer to these values will ensure that it's easier to drop these types of relationships.

SELF-RESPECT AND SELF-CONFIDENCE

"Self-esteem means knowing you are the dream."
Oprah Winfrey

The western culture constantly bombards us with images and information that make us feel inferior physically.

Companies do this that we will buy their product with the hope that it will plug the insecurity that the companies created in the first place. This type of messaging was not part of our heritage as we were too busy with our roles in the tribes.

If we are to move forward we must reject this western concept of beauty and create our own understanding of our individual beauty and value. We are much more than our physical appearance.

We must focus on our usefulness and growing our skills and our capacity for empowerment. The more you get busy and pursue your purpose the more your self-respect and self-confidence will grow and the less you'll care what the world or other people think.

As Beyonce says:

> *"We all have our imperfections. But I'm human, and you know, it's important to concentrate on other qualities besides outer beauty."*

If you are a Christian you must begin to know for yourself that God created you in his image, that every part of you is beautiful.

HONOUR AND INTEGRITY

We must value honour and integrity as women as this is the very thing that keeps us cohesive as a community. We must be able to trust each other and to be able to rely on each other. Our word must be our bond.

I've found that people who practice honouring themselves and others and acting with integrity feel happy inside, as they are acting in the right ways and doing good.

The things that stop people from practicing honour and integrity are laziness and not knowing how to act in an honourable way. Sometimes it's easier to go back on your word but I can guarantee that you will feel bad about yourself when you do this.

Practicing honour and integrity is part of self-love. African tradition emphasised the right ways to do things and there were often punishments for not following these rules. The Christian tradition is very strong on being loyal and honourable to each other. If you want to grow as a human being make these values the core of how you operate and see how much more you love yourself and others love you.

KINDNESS AND GIVING

The western culture emphasises value on self. In order to be happy you must give to yourself and make sure that all of your needs are met.

This is the opposite of the old ways, which value contribution and giving to a community rather than taking.

This difference is one of the fundamental things we need to set right for our relationships and our culture going forward. As per the Haya (Tanzania) proverb, "Many hands make light work."

The truth is that contribution and giving is one of the key ways to make yourself happier. It will also make you feel more a part of the community and less lonely. Yes, there is a point where sometimes people take advantage of a giver but that's where your other values of self-respect and self-love kick in.

Kindness goes hand in hand with giving. Kindness is giving of the heart and seeing people who are going through bad times and walking alongside them. Kindness makes better relationships because people feel cared for and loved. If you are building a community make kindness one of the key values of it. It will stop ego and vice dead in its tracks.

COMMUNITY

At the start of this book, I wrote about finding a new way for Africans in a modern world and after working with African and western communities for a long time I am still of the belief that community is one of the most valuable things we have as humans.

It provides support and makes us less lonely. It gives us boundaries to operate under and identities to relish in. If we are to grow as women we must value and foster community wherever we are.

Yes, community can be imperfect as we are all imperfectly human but it's the one thing we have that draws us together in groups other than work. It should be inclusive of those who wish to also honour our traditions. It's essential for African relationships going forward.

WARRIOR QUEEN

"If I didn't define myself for myself, I would be crunched into other people's fantasies for me and eaten alive."
Audre Lorde, African American Writer

I've put this down as a value as it's a great symbol of the growing strength of women in society and the need to honour the magnificent warrior queen inside each one of us. The woman that stands her ground and that fights for what's important to her, that demands respect that discards those who are toxic to her.

Whenever you are going through anything that's difficult ask yourself what your warrior queen would do. A warrior queen is kind and benevolent but doesn't take being trod on or used. Giving yourself this archetype helps you to move forward with strength.

★ DEFINING YOUR VALUES EXERCISE

Read the above values and write down whether you feel you have manifested each of them in your life. If so, how have you manifested them? Understand how your past has positively influenced your present.

If not then it's time to get serious about manifesting stronger and more positive values. I've counselled women to bring these into their lives and to manifest them fully. Contact me for counselling options or find a powerful female coach or mentor who can help you.

Also become more mindful of how you work with these values in your daily life and how you can take personal responsibility for improving your identity and your actions.

CHAPTER 6

A NEW WAY FOR AFRICAN MEN

---

*"The basic tenet of black consciousness is that the black man must reject all
value systems that seek to make him a foreigner in the country of
his birth and reduce his basic human dignity."*
Steve Biko, Activist

Colonisation has also had a significant effect on our African men. No
longer are many taught the skills to provide for and protect their families.
Instead, they are left to work it out for themselves while their identity is
eroded and their role and position in society becomes confused. Drugs and
crime also overwhelm so many.

At the same time, the emphasis on males having the power is still
there as this was also the way with white cultures until recently. They are
not taught that with power comes responsibility and they must rise up

and live lives of honour and integrity.

In the past, they were taught how to fish, how to hunt, how to build a house for their family, how to farm, how to use their intellect and their strength to ensure that the household survives. Now there's no longer an emphasis on skills and responsibility.

So many are lost and struggling for an identity.

I'm very aware that as I write these words there are also African men that have been taught or have chosen to school themselves in honour, kindness, responsibility and strength. These men are rising up and shouting from the rooftops that there is a new way and that black men can take back their humble power and become warriors once again. But they must do so in a way that now completely honours the women and allows the women to also rise and be warriors for truth and love alongside them. There are key values that I am seeing in the men that are rising up and I want to point them out here.

FAMILY

"A united family eats from the same plate."
Baganda proverb

If a man wishes to embrace his heritage and a modernised future he must value family above all else and choose every day to invest time and focus on his family.

This means that instead of spending time on technology at night he must choose to establish a bonfire of sorts at home where he engages with his children and teaches them the skills and gives them the advice to keep them on track in a modern world that's constantly trying to erode them. This investment in time is very important as it builds trust and community. There are so many benefits if a man chooses to invest in his family. His wife is happier and feels more supported, his children become more confident and understand themselves better, there's greater harmony in the home.

HARD WORK

African men that commit to this value are rising up. As our identities have been confused since colonisation one of the ways to ensure an increase in identity is for the man to commit to working hard so that he can feel better about himself and be more capable of providing for his family.

Hard work is the path through lost identity. It was the way in our communities in Africa, we had to work hard or we would not eat or survive. It must be the way now.

KINDNESS AND GIVING

If a man is kind he will also love. He will think of others and people will love him in turn.

When the world is asking men to be hard and ruthless a man

must make a choice to be kind. This choice will not make him less of a man but a greater man as he will show softness in his strength.

This value of kindness also means that he will treat the woman he is with well as he will feel both empathy and love.

STRENGTH AND RESILIENCE

In the old ways, men were taught strength and resilience. They needed to face fear and overcome it. They could not be called a man until they showed that they had strength in the face of adversity.

Strength is a value and a trait that is built over time. It can be fostered in our sons and daughters by teaching them how to overcome challenges and celebrating when they do. It is now about constantly praising them and encouraging selfishness but encouraging selflessness and giving and seeing strength as something that is employed to help others not you.

Strength can be encouraged in relationships by allowing men to take over and to face the challenges on behalf of the family. We must allow our men to be men and to step up.

CHAPTER 7

A NEW WAY FOR AFRICAN PARENTING AND FAMILIES

————————

*"Train a child the way he should go and make sure you
also go the same way."*
African proverb

*"Start children off on the way they should go, and even when they
are old they will not turn from it."*
Proverbs 22:6

We are seeing across the board a fragmentation of the family unit in African communities. Divorce is on the rise and single parents are struggling to parent their children. This was not the way in the old communities. The family unit was revered as the basis for the community and harmony was extremely important. That's not to say that there wasn't conflicts and issues but fundamentally we must come back to seeing family as a priority, regardless of how stressful our lives are. There are several practices and values that are continuing to erode the family and I'm going to address these one by one. If you are looking to enrich your family unit I encourage you to read through this chapter thoroughly and start to engage with the exercises outlined.

After years of counselling, I believe that change can happen but you must be persistent and constant and know that this will very much be a case of two steps forward one step backward.

Also if you are married decide together that you're going to start implementing practices that will shift the family dynamics and commit to the idea together.

BRING BACK THE BONFIRE

Most nights in Zambia we'd sit around the bonfire after dinner and our parents and other community members would tell us stories that contained wisdom about how to live life.

Many families today have dinner in front of TV or eat dinner together playing with their phones. This means that there's no space at all for parents to guide their children and this only ends up happening when there's a crisis and the child is well on the way to practicing destructive behaviour or being a victim of it.

I'm very aware that this pattern of behaviour is now the norm across the board and parents may struggle to get any cooperation from children to engage during or after dinner.

The fact is that if there's no engagement there's no chance for training, for values to be imparted and the child will get their training and values from society, their friends, and the internet. We must train our children; it's imperative that they receive this so they can understand how to live life.

Many parents these days feel they are too tired from working and leave the babysitting to the television or technology. This may be the case but the value of engaging is far greater than letting your kids learn from everyone else but you and the exercise of establishing a bonfire doesn't need to happen every night, just as regularly as you can make it.

If you bring back the bonfire, the time when the family engages after dinner then you bring back the chance to influence and learn. Obviously, you can't build a bonfire in your living room but there are ways to foster a similar environment. See my tips below.

★ TIPS FOR CREATING A BONFIRE ENVIRONMENT

1. When the children are young make sure the time after dinner is for reading them stories and allowing them to ask questions. Try to avoid technology or television even though at times you'll feel tired. You can always supply books for them that teach valuable lessons to read if you are needing a break, the most important thing is that you're present and they can see that you are there.

2. If the children are older it's going to be harder to establish this pattern of engagement. Society will have already taught disengagement and they'll be engaging in technology. Regardless of this resistance, it's vitally important that you establish a practice of a technology free few hours even once a week. This is more likely to be successful if it's around the dinner table and if something else engages them such as a game or a discussion. You will get complaints but over time your children will begin to value this time as the truth is that they still value your love and connection. This will require effort and consistency from you but know that it's worth it. You want them to come to you in times of crisis and if they have important things that they are trying to work through, providing a bonfire time for them will mean that they'll be more likely to do this as the pattern of family community will be established.

3. I encourage you to go on a holiday with your children where you can create a campfire. Talk to them about the old ways of telling stories around a fire and that this experience will give them insight into the true spirit and experience of Africa and then read or tell them some African American stories.

Also in the evenings, we gathered for the evening show dance called the Gulewamukulu or Nyau dance. You can view this dance on YouTube and enjoy the dance and picture yourself in my village. Show your children

their chief, village headman and the Boma or district they come from
including their paramount chief.

★ A BONFIRE STORY TO SHARE WITH YOUR CHILDREN

I also encourage you to start to connect with the old stories and share
them with your children. There are plenty of African stories on the
internet to choose from and there are books of African stories as well.
You can read them with your children and talk to them about the wisdom
inherent in each one. Here's one of my favourite stories.

Once upon a time, there was a couple that had no children. The woman
spent time lamenting, till one day a fairy came and told her to make a
wish. She said she wanted a baby, so the fairy got some mud and made
a doll, which transformed into a human female baby which the parents
called Mud.

This baby came with instructions that she must not get wet in
the rains. She was to be kept dry by use of an umbrella. If she got wet she
would stop being human and turn into mud or soil. It so happened that
one day the girl forgot the umbrella and she ventured too far from home.
The clouds became dark and turned into nimbus, the ones that bring rain.

When the mother did not see her daughter before the first
drop of rain, she got worried and started calling out for her daughter.
She sang a song that went like this: "Chamudothiwe chamudothiwe

thawamvula, chamudothiwe, chamudothiwe thawamvula, yaya mwananga chamudothiwe thawamvula, chamudothiwe thawamvula."(The translation of this is: Daughter made from soil, run away from the rain can't you see its raining, please run and come to me and I will keep you safe.)

She called and cried and ran like crazy looking for her daughter for she knew what would happen and she loved Mud very much. Then the heavens opened and it rained cats and dogs.

Mud had ventured into thick forest with friends and she had forgotten about the time and the instructions given to her by her mother. When it poured she remembered that she would turn to mud and she tried to run as fast as the fastest man in the world, but to no avail. Just when she was about to reunite with her mother whose voice was hoarse from calling she melted and turned back into soil.

The fairy appeared and said, "Well I had helped but it appears there was lack of keeping to instructions."

The moral of the story It is important for children to listen and do what the parents says otherwise there will be consequences and sometimes a life can be lost, or one can be imprisoned due to bad behaviour. Also, parents should continue to reinforce teachings about values, wise behaviour, and morals, to save a life from ruin.

Telling a story is often the best way that children can learn about how to live good and wise lives. After telling the story, ask the children what they have learnt.

ENCOURAGE RESPECT

*"It is the duty of children to wait on elders and
not the elders on children."*
Kenyan proverb

There's an emerging pattern in western society where the child ends up ruling the household. The parents spend all their time praising and serving the child and they believe that this will produce a productive and successful member of society.

Years of tradition in African culture has shown that the reverse is true. The older members of the family have the wisdom gained through years and the child is an empty and naïve vessel that needs to be trained and guided. Children in our communities were taught to respect their elders. As I've previously mentioned this was to the extent that they would kneel in their presence, a physical representation of this respect. Obviously kneeling is not accepted in western culture but many more traditional families use less obvious signs of respect such as a bowing of the head whenever an elder is in the room.

In many ways, though this strong physical gesture helped to reinforce that the child was yet to learn the ways of the adult and this also helped the child and the adult to establish very strong roles and identities.

Western culture encourages individualism and lack of respect for authority and that can break down identities and devalue all involved. Respect needs to be taught from a young age and it's very important for the children to understand the value of respecting their parents and elders in that this will ensure that they have better training and become more respectful and better quality adults.

Nowadays you will need to explain to your children that your culture is different to the western culture in this respect so that they understand. Also, you will need to reinforce and be consistent with ensuring that children respect your decisions even though this will be tougher than giving in.

You also have a responsibility to make sure that your decisions are fair and just and not just a result of your own ego and selfishness. Respect cannot be gained through violence; it must be gained through love. Your child will know how to act because you showed them how to act. Never underestimate the influence of your behaviour on your children.

Building respect in a family ensures harmony in the long run and helps everyone understand who he or she is within the unit. It can also save lives and stop children from falling into ways that can hurt them such as drug and alcohol abuse.

If the unit is ruled by the children this can only result in chaos and their naive decisions have no schooling or wisdom.

★ WAYS THAT CHILDREN AND YOUNG ADULTS CAN SHOW RESPECT THAT IS APPROPRIATE FOR WESTERN CULTURE AND DRAW FROM OUR AFRICAN CULTURE

Children and young adults can start showing practices of respect in the following ways:

- Ensure that if you are meeting a senior member of the family that you dress formally.
- Work on dressing in a self-respecting manner to show pride in your appearance and consideration for others. If clothes are falling off you or you are exposing a lot of skin it's a sign that you are not valuing yourself as a human being.
- Speak politely to parents or older people.
- Say "please" and "thank you."
- Stand up and give a seat to those less able to stand such as the elderly or pregnant women in any situation.
- Understand that you do not have permission to throw a tantrum in public places and embarrass parents or seniors in the community.
- Do not pick up or use anything at someone else's house without asking permission.
- Do not talk back or walk away when adults are talking to you.
- In African culture, we have the practice of not looking adults directly in the eye. The practice is to look once to show you are listening and

then remove eye contact. A head slightly bowed shows respect for the parents.

- Swearing is not allowed in the family unit as it's a device that can be easily used to disrespect people.

REDUCE TECHNOLOGY

African people are not the only ones struggling with the incredible influx of technology into our lives. Families all over the world are starting to suffer communication breakdown as they become more absorbed in technology than in building relationships. It's now common for people to eat food while also browsing or chatting to others on their phones.

Technology is also reducing attention spans and causing children to become less able to focus on tasks or at school.

Social media is also very addictive as one can get social approval quickly just through posting and this has been proven to set off positive chemicals in the brain.

The inverse is also true where young people feel isolated and even bullied by others on the net.

Many parents are giving technology to their children from a very young age as a form of babysitting. I'd strongly discourage this as it means that the child will have little capacity for focus and concentration and will also fail to notice the world outside of the screen. Young children learn by looking at things so make sure the things they are looking at are of the real world, not the world inside of a computer. Teach them to construct their own play and not be passive to a computer screen.

I've little doubt that there will be a slow recognition of the impacts of this wave of technology and the fact that humans and families are becoming more fragmented. Teachers are already starting to complain that the new wave of students that have been raised on technology have issues with attention spans and get bored very easily. You really don't want this for your child.

One of the great things about living in communities years ago was that the distraction from life came from each other, from the fun we had, from the work we had to do, and from the stories we told. We were more present and therefore more able to react and deal with whatever came along.

In response to the influx of technology, many people are starting to go technology free for periods. This helps to reduce the addiction, increases focus and also helps people to live more in the present. Families can also adopt this for periods of time to ensure that family members are looking up from their phones and starting to learn how to relate to others.

★ TIPS FOR TECHNOLOGY DETOX

1. Start low and slow with your technology detox for your family. Try for a few hours one night of the week where you turn off the TV and all devices. Think of an activity to do during this time that

shows the children that the time without technology can actually be fun. Show them that they can find stimulation without their phones.

2. Talk to your children about how this experience made them feel, what they think they can do during the time of technology detox that will interest them. Give them the power to find and construct their own stimulus.

3. Exercise in nature is one of the best ways to detox from technology. The child gets the same positive endorphins and also feels fitter and more able. Find a park or nature reserve on a weekend and take them for long walks. Get them out and away from the computer.

4. Try tapping into their creative side by giving them arts and craft projects to do that stimulate their brains. Get them to write their own stories that they can tell around your bonfire nights.

TEACH SKILLS

In the old ways, it was absolutely essential that parents and community members passed on skills to the younger generation. This ensured the continuation of the tribe but it also increased the confidence of the child in that they felt capable of fulfilling their role in the community.

In the western culture, many parents leave it up to the schools to teach the child skills and take a little responsibility for it themselves. This reduces the relationship between the child and the parent but it also means that the child doesn't know that the parent is the one to come to when they have issues.

Parents must take back their role from our culture and start to become teachers again. I'm not just talking about teaching about manners; I'm talking about teaching practical and essential skills.

Even a hundred years ago in western culture parents taught their children how to do practical things and this gave the child more confidence and helped them to grow up and become more responsible for themselves.

When we grew up in Africa my siblings and I often helped Mum and Dad on the farm. My younger brother learnt how to heard cattle, how to attach cows to the plough for tilling the land including how to train the cows to maintain a straight line and how to teach the cows not to graze while on the job.

He got a hand from his youngest brother who lived full-time with our parents. They milked the cows and brought the milk to Mum, who prepared our favourite morning dish: porridge with milk made from roller meal, with all its nutrients intact. This brings a smile and sadness to my countenance as our parents are no more, but memories linger.

My eldest sister is now the matriarch of the family as almost all the elders are deceased from Dad's side. Mum left a lot of great grandchildren and the ones who are being born will have to look up to my eldest sister for information on the family tree. I normally ask her to fill in the blanks about how Mum and Dad became entrepreneurs in their own right. My elder sister took up the role of father and mother when Dad died. She provided for us and supported us to finish our schooling and become independent. She had sewing skills, which she was taught from my Dad. She's a very talented clothing designer. At one point she employed workers to help her while she worked her 8-5 job to supplement her income.

My Mum was a great potter. I remember going to the river with her to gather special clay, which was grey in color. After she created the pots she'd burn them and one day later they would be ready.

One of the skills I was taught is crocheting. It comes in handy when I need a quick buck or decorate my living room.

The value of skills cannot be overemphasized; it's a necessity.

The teaching of skills from parents to children is being eroded and we need to take back this tradition. When you teach your children skills their confidence and self-esteem also increases. Teaching skills benefit everyone. But how do you begin to teach skills to your children? Here are some tips.

★ TIPS FOR TEACHING SKILLS

1. Take some time out from family life and document the kinds of practical skills you have. It might be cooking, fixing things, painting, and drawing, building things, anything that is practical and makes life better for you. If you don't have any skills and just

spend your life in an office and coming home then I want you to start to think about a practical skill you could acquire.

2. If you are only just learning a practical skill yourself then ask your child or children to learn it with you. If you are already skilled then set aside some time once every week or two weeks to teach the skill to your child. See if you cannot attach a gender role to the skill if your son is interested in cooking then teach him how to cook. Every skill gained means greater confidence and a better sense of self for the child.

3. At first, your child may be resistant but be patient and persevere. Show them the benefits of learning this skill. For example, if it's cooking teach them just how delicious their food can be.

4. Be kind during this process. Don't berate things if they don't do things correctly; tell them that mistakes are the only path to learning and growing.

5. The next step once they've started to gain confidence is to ask them to use this skill by themselves or with minimal help from you. Have them try and then discuss with them how they can improve. Keep encouraging them to engage.

6. Don't give up on this. Make sure that you are persistent. Give the child the support he or she needs to succeed and become skilful.

7. Once you've done this try teaching another skill and stick with it until the child feels confident.

BE ENTHUSIASTIC ABOUT EDUCATION

Education will change your children's lives full stop. It will be the key to them living successful lives. Our culture was all about education and we must continue this tradition through using the educational facilities created by the west. We must see education as one of the top priorities in our families so that our families can survive and our children can obtain opportunities. If our children receive both skills and education they will become a force to be reckoned with and will have more confidence and a greater sense of identity. Also start early and teach them about entrepreneurship and self-reliance.

WALK IN GOOD CIRCLES AND TEACH THE SAME

The environment your child grows up in depends on the immediate environment of your home and also who you associate with.

If you spend time with toxic people your child will replicate the same behaviour. If the people that surround you put you down and try to suppress you then you must move on from them for the sake of your children.

Find circles and a community that is supportive and loving and people that are honourable and your child will see only this type of behaviour as the norm.

Teach your children the consequences of hanging with the wrong crowd and encourage them to pursue education and community rather than destructive friends.

CHANGE HABITS

"It is the habit that a child forms at home, that follows them to their marriage."
Nigerian proverb

Changing habits is the key to everything else working? Unfortunately, we've slipped into a state where we have habits that have come from other cultures and from a modernised world and some of them are beneficial and some are not. In order to make positive change within a family unit, the parents must be invested in giving time and focus to the change and also must work on changing their own habits.

For example, if you feel exhausted after coming home from work and just want to sit in front of TV with a TV dinner for yourself and your children and if you don't have enough passion for change then no change is going to happen.

It takes three months to break a habit and this applies to both yourself and your children. When you commit to building more relationship into your family then you must commit to being resilient and seeing things through. One thing I can say is that you will feel great when the change is finally built into your everyday life and doesn't feel foreign but becomes a habit in itself.

If you want to change habits also build in positive events or reinforcement throughout the process. See the change as a series of steps that are celebrated at the end of each step. Make sure you persist because the harmony and happiness of your family is at stake. The first few weeks or even months of habit changing are going to be tough but it will get easier.

CHAPTER 8

WE MUST BUILD OUR COMMUNITIES TO SUPPORT OUR RELATIONSHIPS

———————

"There can be no greater gift than that of giving one's time and energy to help others without expecting anything in return."
Nelson Mandela

Our communities sustained us as a people for thousands of years. They were the place that helped us to establish our identity, they had rules that set boundaries for behaviour and they provided support for the adults and the children. It truly did take a village to raise a child as the African proverb says. Our communities also helped us to connect to the divine how we saw it.

When the white man came he didn't see the value of our

communities, and he slowly but surely dismantled them and told us that our ways were primitive and we needed to follow the ways of the west. A Nigerian proverb says, "When the roots of a tree begin to decay, it spreads death to the branches." Unfortunately, this is what is happening in our communities and many of us are lonely and disconnected from each other and the positive aspects of our traditions. Many of our youth aren't taught how to behave, many adults are too busy being busy and many are simply lost.

If we truly want our relationships to thrive we must do everything we can to bring back community so that our youth are taught how to behave, our parents and marriages are supported, and our men and women can grow and thrive.

Communities are not perfect, our African communities were not perfect, but it's 100% essential for the sake of ourselves, our relationships and our children that we foster community.

If you are a part of a community or want to start to grow one and meet with your brothers and sisters here's my tips for growing communities.

START SMALL

If you are looking to build a community start with something small such a small group that meets regularly. The important thing is to create something that can be sustained over years rather than months. Don't have the expectation of numbers but of the quality of relationships and engagement.

FOCUS ON SKILLS

Our culture was very much about training people in skills. Building a community that is determined to learn more about a subject or a series of subjects not only honours our heritage but it also advances the knowledge and success of each individual member of the community and the community as a whole. Skills based communities could include training in just about anything. We've had a lot of success in building a community around skills for starting and sustaining a business venture.

See what skills are lacking and establish a community to build those skills.

ASSIGN ROLES

It's vitally important that leadership roles are established in a growing community so that harmony is maintained. The best thing to do is to establish these roles at the outset so that people know who the leaders are and who to go to for support or information.

This also ensures there's some mechanism for your leadership to be accountable to reduce ego and manipulation.

TEACH AND HONOUR OUR CULTURE

Make sure you build in some aspect of the community to teach and honour our culture. Whether it is that you gather for traditional food after a meeting or you impart cultural information or conduct rituals as part of the format of the gatherings.

This will give your communities a sense of depth and place and help you and your children to truly understand where you came from and the traditions that have sustained your ancestors.

If you are part of a Christian community find ways to share both the Christian customs and the African customs. Honour both.

For example, my cousin sings in a choir called the Levite Choir. It is made up of seventh day Adventist who loves to sing for the Lord and evangelise about Christ in music. They meet most Sabbath afternoons to practice. Often times they are invited to minister to congregation through its music. I accompany them from time to time. They have been invited outside UK to sing including the USA General conference, headquarters of seventh-day church. Any ethnic tribe is welcome and a majority of the members are Zambians. There are also some from Zimbabwe and the Caribbean. Traditional food is shared and family life is fostered. Children are educated in the traditional values including self-esteem, confidence boosting and how to respect the elders. The choir sings in nursing homes sometimes and on New Year's Eve, they minister in Oxford Street. The choir also perform acts of charity.

There is also another charity organisation called UK zaf. Zambia Adventist Fellowship. All Zambians in the Diaspora gather 2 or 3 times a year, to worship God, with one accord to worship the Zambian way. This fosters unity and togetherness. Women are called upon to impart knowledge to a bride to be via bridal showers to those whose parents want to continue with traditional marriage teachings.

ACCEPT THOSE WHO WANT TO KNOW OUR CULTURE OR WHO ARE PART OF MIXED MARRIAGES

As many of us are part of western society a number of us will marry men or women from another culture. If these people are open and willing to accept our culture and our customs then we must accept them and teach them our ways. This will ensure that their children are educated in both cultures and will be able to honour and understand our ways. It's better to be friendly and open than turn away from people with mixed marriages.

ESTABLISH STRONG DISPUTE RESOLUTION POLICIES AND PROCEDURES

Make sure you document how your community will handle disputes that will most certainly come up during the life of a community. This is also the way of our ancestors, in that everyone knew how to handle a dispute. Make sure you have this written down and you clearly communicate this to your community members. The bible too has procedures to follow when people have a dispute.

BE CONSISTENT AND RESILIENT

A deep and supportive community takes years to foster as people need time to get to know each other. Before you start any community make sure you are in it for the long term or have systems in place so that the community can be sustained if you leave. If we are to bring back our communities they cannot be a flash in the pan, they must be in it for the long term.

BE PREPARED TO ADJUST AS THE COMMUNITY GROWS

As the community grows there may be changes to the needs of community members and in the objective of the group. Be prepared to keep the foundational values of the group and continue to foster the traditions but be prepared to be flexible to keep the community harmonious. Practice brainstorming new ideas to keep the community members interested and engaged.

LOOK OUT FOR AND SUPPORT EACH OTHER

I've left this to the last but it's the most important. As Africans with a strong history of community we must be the uncles and aunties, the brothers and sisters for each other. Within our communities, we must encourage people to express how they are feeling and we must also watch and listen for signs that another member of the community is going through hard times.

Western civilisation is now used to living separately but we have a choice as to whether we want to go down that path or become part of a community.

Sure there are times when community members will be too much in your face and you'll want time out but wouldn't you rather that than having reduced support and often loneliness?

Make sure that the communities you foster also respect people and give them space when needed but also be deliberate about helping each other. Offer to look after children if the parents need a break, bring people food and company; help the members of your community to become better versions of themselves.

As the bible says, "Love one another. As I have loved you, so you must love one another." John 13:34.

The Kenyan proverb also says, "People who love one another do not dwell on each other's mistakes." Mistakes will be a part of a community but they should not destroy it.

Love changes people; it makes them better. Use your communities to love one another, to forgive each other's mistakes and to bring back your tree, your roots, and your branches.

ENDORSEMENT

———————

There's no doubt in my mind that our grandparents came to this earth with a lot of knowledge and wisdom.

I am sure you will agree that your grandparents always seem to be the ones with real life changing answers that seem to come from an insight that we cannot see with the naked eyes.

Africa is what we call the motherland or the cradle of humanity and this is not just an old saying, this is where our people originated from, where we lived as nature intended, where years old tradition were rooted and founded in the times of old.

No wonder we are so full of rich history, our parents, their parents and their parents, parents were the ones who studied and learned the way of life and passed it down to generations. In those days people studied humans and made the best of every situation. Just remember from the beginning of time it was normal for women to stand up to give birth, why? Well because it was only natural for a woman to bear down and push her child out, but then came the start of what other cultures perceived as the better way (laying down) but really it was for their own selfishness why women started laying on the backs to give birth which made the pain twice as hard and twice as long.

This was definitely the start of loosing our culture and the depletion of good quality deep rooted knowledge that kept a family and community together. Everything was done with a meaning, down to naming your child, they were given names with meanings and nowadays we give a child a name because it sounds great, people not actually knowing that names are powerful.

In those days it took a village to raise a child and the village were actually responsible for every child even if they were not blood related. This cascaded to parts of the Caribbean and they too adopted this attitude, if your child did something wrong the village (or community) had the right to chastise your child without any repercussions, (but not now, you would be in deep trouble).

Reading this book brings back some of the memories my parents brought with them to the UK. But having been born and raised in a society there you are not allowed to scold your child leaves us with children that have no manners, relationships that give up on each other quickly because it is easy. Back in Africa marriage was important and not to be taken lightly, it was a joint venture with the community and of course both families and it was for life not like these days you can get married several times.

Thinking of my parents who are from the Caribbean they are almost 90 years old and have been together for over 60 years, they took their marriage vowels seriously for better or for worse, for richer or for poorer, no matter what they stuck together. These traditions were instilled in them from their fore parents from way back in Africa.

If your relationship was in trouble you will find solace from the elders in the African community who would have been watching you grow up from young, seen your marriage, know your families and of course came from your community. Nowadays you would go to a relationship counsellor who knows nothing about your culture or how you were raised so how can they give you the correct advice. Our African culture is important to be kept and passed on to the next generation.

Even the stories of old are important because each story is a fable with a real life meaning that could change your world.

This book can definitely be used as a guide to help you heal your relationship, get a better understanding of what is essential in a relationship and of course how best to serve each other which ultimately will give you a long lasting and loving relationship with your spouse.

When you find that love of your life, you want to ensure that you enjoy each other, you want to please and serve each other and of course you want to live a life of love, this book will serve as a tool that will ensure you can find a way to not only understand each other but also to ensure that you live a happy and fruitful life together just as nature intended it to be.

It was not by chance that you stumbled across such information so don't allow this book to be shelf development, allow it to speak into your life and allow it to be the change that you need in order to live an extremely happy and fulfilled life with your chosen life time partner.

Allow this book to speak into your life and be the change that you are searching for.

SONIA POLEON

BA (Hon), HNC, Dip | Radio Personality, Speaker & Consultant | Award Winning Author of The Love List

ABOUT THE AUTHOR

Valerie Muzelenga was born in Zambia in Mufulira Town. She went to Mufulira High School and trained as a nurse at Kitwe school of Nursing In 1982. Later she did her Midwifery at Ndola School of Midwifery 1985. She is an avid reader, marriage and relationship counsellor, public speaker and Co- Author of an anthology Formerly Known as Pain to Purpose, now Rebranded Journey to Purpose.

Valerie is the Former chairperson of Amaka Yabwingi networking Ltd, Women Department, London Branch. She specialized in teaching women the four pillars of Amakayabwingi network and capacity build help businesses to Network. These four pillars; promotion, education, linking, and innovation are also her guiding force as she embarks on her journey of innovation.

Valerie has been giving back to her community since she started her adulthood journey in Zambia. There, she trained and worked as a Registered Nurse and Midwife for fourteen years before moving to Botswana where she worked for the Unified Local Government in a similar position. In 2005, Valerie moved to England and started doing marriage talks and health promotion to small groups of women and men. Having spent most of her life watching her mother empower young women to speak up and voice their concerns, Valerie developed superior competence and passion for advocating for women and teaching them to tap into their God-given inner strength, beauty, and purpose. This passion drove her to seek further certification. Now, she is a qualified counsellor of the prevention of transmission of HIV/AIDS from mother to the unborn child. Recently, she successfully concluded an Advanced Diploma in Prevention of HIV/AIDS and STDs. She is a qualified trainer- With a certificate in PTTLS, Preparing to teach in the lifelong sector.

Valerie is an overcomer. She has earned this title after she conquered depression which tried to hold her hostage after she experienced three deaths in succession and a violent plane crash for which nobody viewing was held. In addition to that, she overcame her fear of viewing dead bodies. Valerie will soon be releasing her book Gone which captures some of her journey and
triumphs.

Valerie places great energy in supporting family and friends and living in harmony. She will continue to focus on supporting women to have enriched and blissful marriages that are grounded in love and are destruction-proof from the vile of this world.

Connect with Valerie. She's waiting to have a talk with you and guide you through your marriage
and relationship counselling.

Facebook:
Valerie Muzelenga

Facebook Group:
African Relationships, in the 21st century.

Website:
https://www.valeriecounselling.com/

www.ingramcontent.com/pod-product-compliance
Lightning Source LLC
Chambersburg PA
CBHW072210280526
45788CB00002B/962